45 Easter Recipes for Home

By: Kelly Johnson

Table of Contents

Appetizers:

- Deviled Eggs with Smoked Salmon
- Spring Vegetable Platter with Dip
- Asparagus and Prosciutto Bundles
- Mini Quiches with Spinach and Feta
- Caprese Skewers with Cherry Tomatoes and Mozzarella

Main Courses:

- Herb-Roasted Leg of Lamb
- Honey Glazed Ham
- Roast Chicken with Lemon and Rosemary
- Baked Salmon with Dill Sauce
- Vegetarian Stuffed Peppers

Sides:

- Scalloped Potatoes
- Glazed Carrots with Maple Syrup
- Lemon Garlic Roasted Asparagus
- Creamy Spinach and Artichoke Casserole
- Wild Rice Pilaf with Mushrooms

Salads:

- Spring Mix Salad with Strawberries and Goat Cheese
- Greek Salad with Feta and Kalamata Olives
- Roasted Beet and Arugula Salad
- Citrus Avocado Salad
- Broccoli Salad with Bacon and Cranberries

Breads:

- Hot Cross Buns
- Easter Braided Bread

- Garlic and Herb Dinner Rolls
- Spinach and Feta Stuffed Bread
- Carrot and Walnut Bread

Desserts:

- Easter Bunny Sugar Cookies
- Carrot Cake with Cream Cheese Frosting
- Lemon Tart with Raspberry Sauce
- Chocolate Nest Cupcakes
- Coconut Cream Pie

Easter Egg Treats:

- Chocolate Peanut Butter Eggs
- Marbled Easter Egg Truffles
- Speckled Easter Egg Cake Pops
- Easter Egg-Shaped Sugar Cookies
- Almond Butter Easter Eggs

Drinks:

- Sparkling Raspberry Lemonade
- Easter Punch with Fruit Ice Ring
- Minty Lime Cooler
- Carrot Orange Ginger Smoothie
- Non-Alcoholic Easter Egg Punch

Brunch:

- Quiche Lorraine
- Blueberry Pancakes
- Eggs Benedict with Hollandaise Sauce
- Smoked Salmon Bagels
- Fruit Salad with Honey-Lime Dressing

Appetizers:

Deviled Eggs with Smoked Salmon

Ingredients:

- 6 hard-boiled eggs, peeled and cut in half lengthwise
- 2 tablespoons mayonnaise
- 1 teaspoon Dijon mustard
- 1 teaspoon white wine vinegar
- Salt and pepper, to taste
- 2 ounces smoked salmon, finely chopped
- Fresh dill, for garnish

Instructions:

Prepare Eggs:
- Cut the hard-boiled eggs in half lengthwise. Carefully remove the yolks and place them in a bowl.

Make Filling:
- Mash the egg yolks with a fork. Add mayonnaise, Dijon mustard, white wine vinegar, salt, and pepper. Mix until smooth and well combined.

Add Smoked Salmon:
- Fold in the finely chopped smoked salmon into the yolk mixture. Ensure it is evenly distributed.

Fill Egg Whites:
- Spoon or pipe the yolk and salmon mixture back into the hollowed egg whites.

Garnish:
- Garnish each deviled egg with a small piece of smoked salmon and fresh dill.

Chill and Serve:
- Refrigerate the deviled eggs for at least 30 minutes to allow the flavors to meld. Serve chilled.

Enjoy:
- Arrange the deviled eggs on a serving platter and enjoy this delightful and elegant appetizer.

Tips:

- Presentation: To create a more elegant presentation, use a piping bag or a plastic sandwich bag with the corner snipped off to fill the egg whites.
- Make-Ahead: Prepare the deviled eggs a few hours in advance and keep them refrigerated until ready to serve.

These Deviled Eggs with Smoked Salmon make for an impressive and flavorful addition to any appetizer spread, whether it's for Easter, brunch, or any special occasion. Enjoy the combination of creamy eggs and the rich, smoky flavor of the salmon!

Spring Vegetable Platter with Dip

Spring Vegetable Platter:

Ingredients:

- 1 bunch of fresh asparagus, trimmed
- 1 cup cherry tomatoes
- 1 cucumber, sliced
- 1 bell pepper (assorted colors), sliced
- 1 bunch of radishes, trimmed and halved
- Baby carrots
- Snap peas or sugar snap peas

Instructions:

Blanch Asparagus:
- Bring a pot of water to boil. Blanch the asparagus for 2-3 minutes until bright green. Transfer to an ice bath to cool quickly.

Arrange Vegetables:
- Arrange all the vegetables on a large serving platter in an appealing and colorful manner.

Spring-themed Design:
- Get creative with the arrangement, perhaps forming a flower pattern or organizing the veggies by color.

Serve Chilled:
- Keep the platter in the refrigerator until ready to serve for a refreshing and crisp presentation.

Herb Yogurt Dip:

Ingredients:

- 1 cup Greek yogurt
- 1 tablespoon fresh dill, chopped
- 1 tablespoon fresh chives, chopped
- 1 tablespoon fresh parsley, chopped
- 1 clove garlic, minced
- Juice of half a lemon
- Salt and pepper, to taste

Instructions:

> Prepare Dip:
> - In a bowl, combine Greek yogurt, chopped dill, chives, parsley, minced garlic, and lemon juice.
>
> Season:
> - Season the dip with salt and pepper. Mix well to incorporate the herbs evenly.
>
> Chill:
> - Allow the dip to chill in the refrigerator for at least 30 minutes before serving to let the flavors meld.
>
> Serve:
> - Spoon the herb yogurt dip into a small bowl and place it in the center of the vegetable platter.
>
> Enjoy:
> - Serve the Spring Vegetable Platter with Herb Yogurt Dip and enjoy the fresh and crisp flavors.

Tips:

- Variety: Feel free to add other spring vegetables like blanched green beans, baby zucchini, or colorful bell pepper strips.
- Dip Substitutes: Hummus, tzatziki, or your favorite dressing can be used as an alternative dip.

This Spring Vegetable Platter with Herb Yogurt Dip is not only visually appealing but also a healthy and delicious option for any springtime gathering or celebration. Enjoy the vibrant colors and flavors of the season!

Asparagus and Prosciutto Bundles

Ingredients:

- 1 bunch of fresh asparagus spears
- Olive oil
- Salt and black pepper, to taste
- Thin slices of prosciutto (1 slice per 3-4 asparagus spears)
- Balsamic glaze, for drizzling (optional)

Instructions:

Preheat Oven:
- Preheat your oven to 400°F (200°C).

Prepare Asparagus:
- Trim the tough ends from the asparagus spears. Toss them in olive oil and season with salt and black pepper.

Bundle Asparagus:
- Take 3-4 asparagus spears and wrap them with a slice of prosciutto. Repeat until all asparagus spears are bundled.

Roast Asparagus Bundles:
- Place the asparagus and prosciutto bundles on a baking sheet. Roast in the preheated oven for about 10-12 minutes or until the asparagus is tender and the prosciutto is crispy.

Drizzle with Balsamic Glaze (Optional):
- If desired, drizzle the bundles with balsamic glaze for added flavor.

Serve:
- Arrange the asparagus and prosciutto bundles on a serving platter. Serve warm.

Tips:

- Variations: You can sprinkle grated Parmesan or Pecorino cheese over the asparagus before roasting for an extra layer of flavor.
- Grill Option: Instead of roasting, you can also grill the asparagus bundles for a smoky flavor.

These asparagus and prosciutto bundles are not only a tasty appetizer but also a visually appealing addition to your spring or Easter table. Enjoy the combination of the crisp prosciutto and tender asparagus!

Mini Quiches with Spinach and Feta

Ingredients:

- 1 package (about 12) pre-made mini tart shells or phyllo cups
- 1 cup fresh spinach, chopped
- 1/2 cup feta cheese, crumbled
- 4 large eggs
- 1/2 cup milk or cream
- Salt and pepper, to taste
- 1/4 teaspoon nutmeg (optional)
- Olive oil for sautéing spinach

Instructions:

Preheat Oven:
- Preheat your oven to 375°F (190°C).

Prepare Tart Shells:
- If using pre-made tart shells, arrange them on a baking sheet according to package instructions. If using phyllo cups, place them on a baking sheet.

Sauté Spinach:
- In a pan, heat a small amount of olive oil over medium heat. Add chopped spinach and sauté until wilted. Remove from heat and let it cool.

Fill Tart Shells:
- Evenly distribute the sautéed spinach and crumbled feta among the tart shells.

Prepare Egg Mixture:
- In a bowl, whisk together eggs, milk or cream, salt, pepper, and nutmeg (if using).

Pour Egg Mixture:
- Pour the egg mixture over the spinach and feta in each tart shell, filling almost to the top.

Bake:
- Bake in the preheated oven for 15-18 minutes or until the quiches are set and the edges are golden brown.

Cool and Serve:
- Allow the mini quiches to cool for a few minutes before serving.

Optional Garnish:
- Garnish with additional crumbled feta or a sprinkle of fresh chopped herbs if desired.

Tips:

- Customize Fillings: Feel free to add ingredients like sautéed mushrooms, diced tomatoes, or caramelized onions for extra flavor.
- Make-Ahead: These mini quiches can be made ahead and reheated before serving.

These Mini Quiches with Spinach and Feta are not only delicious but also visually appealing. They're perfect for serving at brunch, as appetizers, or as a part of your Easter or springtime spread. Enjoy the savory goodness in every bite!

Caprese Skewers with Cherry Tomatoes and Mozzarella

Ingredients:

- Cherry tomatoes
- Fresh mozzarella balls (bocconcini)
- Fresh basil leaves
- Balsamic glaze
- Extra virgin olive oil
- Salt and black pepper, to taste
- Wooden skewers

Instructions:

Prepare Ingredients:
- Wash the cherry tomatoes and pat them dry. Drain any excess liquid from the mozzarella balls. Pick fresh basil leaves.

Assemble Skewers:
- Thread a cherry tomato onto a wooden skewer, followed by a mozzarella ball and a basil leaf. Repeat the pattern until each skewer is filled.

Arrange on Serving Platter:
- Arrange the assembled Caprese skewers on a serving platter.

Drizzle with Balsamic Glaze:
- Drizzle balsamic glaze over the skewers. You can also use a toothpick to create a balsamic drizzle pattern.

Season with Olive Oil, Salt, and Pepper:
- Lightly drizzle extra virgin olive oil over the skewers. Season with a pinch of salt and a grind of black pepper to taste.

Serve:
- Serve the Caprese skewers immediately or refrigerate until ready to serve.

Tips:

- Freshness Matters: Use the freshest ingredients for the best flavor. Look for ripe cherry tomatoes and high-quality fresh mozzarella.
- Variations: For a different presentation, you can arrange the ingredients on a platter without skewering them.

These Caprese Skewers with Cherry Tomatoes and Mozzarella are not only visually appealing but also a delicious and light appetizer. Enjoy the burst of flavors from the sweet tomatoes, creamy mozzarella, and aromatic basil!

Main Courses:

Herb-Roasted Leg of Lamb

Ingredients:

- 1 leg of lamb (about 5-6 pounds)
- 4 cloves garlic, minced
- 2 tablespoons fresh rosemary, chopped
- 2 tablespoons fresh thyme, chopped
- 1 tablespoon fresh mint, chopped
- 1/4 cup olive oil
- Salt and black pepper, to taste
- 1 cup red wine (optional)
- 1 cup beef or vegetable broth

Instructions:

Preheat Oven:
- Preheat your oven to 375°F (190°C).

Prepare the Leg of Lamb:
- Pat the leg of lamb dry with paper towels. Make small incisions all over the lamb with a knife.

Make Herb Paste:
- In a small bowl, combine minced garlic, chopped rosemary, thyme, mint, olive oil, salt, and black pepper to create an herb paste.

Rub Herb Paste:
- Rub the herb paste all over the leg of lamb, making sure to get it into the incisions.

Place in Roasting Pan:
- Place the seasoned leg of lamb in a roasting pan, fat side up.

Roast:
- Roast in the preheated oven for about 20 minutes per pound for medium-rare or longer if you prefer it more well-done. Use a meat thermometer to check for doneness; it should register 135°F (57°C) for medium-rare, 145°F (63°C) for medium, and 160°F (71°C) for well-done.

Baste and Add Liquid:
- Baste the lamb with its juices every 30 minutes. If desired, pour red wine and broth into the roasting pan to enhance flavors.

Rest:
- Once cooked to your liking, remove the lamb from the oven and let it rest for 15-20 minutes before carving.

Carve and Serve:
- Carve the herb-roasted leg of lamb into slices and serve with the pan juices.

Tips:

- Accompaniments: Serve the herb-roasted leg of lamb with roasted vegetables, mashed potatoes, or a side of mint sauce.
- Cooking Time: Cooking times may vary based on your oven and the size of the leg of lamb, so it's essential to use a meat thermometer for accuracy.

This herb-roasted leg of lamb is sure to be a showstopper at your dinner table, with its aromatic herb crust and tender, juicy meat. Enjoy this classic and elegant dish!

Honey Glazed Ham

Ingredients:

- 1 bone-in, fully-cooked ham (about 7-8 pounds)
- 1 cup honey
- 1/2 cup Dijon mustard
- 1/2 cup brown sugar, packed
- 1/4 cup apple cider vinegar
- 1 teaspoon ground cloves
- 1 teaspoon ground cinnamon

Instructions:

Preheat Oven:
- Preheat your oven to 325°F (163°C).

Prepare the Ham:
- Remove the ham from its packaging and place it in a large roasting pan, cut side down.

Score the Ham:
- Using a sharp knife, score the surface of the ham in a diamond pattern, making cuts about 1/2-inch deep.

Make Glaze:
- In a saucepan over medium heat, combine honey, Dijon mustard, brown sugar, apple cider vinegar, ground cloves, and ground cinnamon. Stir until the mixture is well combined and the sugar is dissolved.

Apply Glaze:
- Brush a generous amount of the honey glaze over the entire surface of the ham, ensuring it gets into the scored cuts.

Bake:
- Cover the ham with aluminum foil and bake in the preheated oven for about 1 hour.

Baste:
- Every 20-30 minutes, baste the ham with the pan juices and additional glaze.

Final Glaze:
- During the last 15-20 minutes of baking, uncover the ham and apply a final layer of the honey glaze. This will create a shiny and caramelized finish.

Check for Doneness:

- Use a meat thermometer to check the internal temperature of the ham. It should register at least 140°F (60°C).

Rest and Serve:
- Allow the ham to rest for about 15 minutes before carving. Slice and serve with the pan juices.

Tips:

- Choosing Ham: You can use a bone-in or boneless fully-cooked ham for this recipe. Adjust the cooking time accordingly.
- Leftovers: Use leftover honey-glazed ham for sandwiches, soups, or omelets.

This honey-glazed ham is sure to be a crowd-pleaser with its sweet and savory flavors. Enjoy this festive and comforting dish during your special occasions!

Roast Chicken with Lemon and Rosemary

Ingredients:

- 1 whole chicken (about 4-5 pounds)
- 1 lemon, halved
- 4-5 sprigs of fresh rosemary
- 4 cloves of garlic, peeled and smashed
- 2 tablespoons olive oil
- Salt and black pepper, to taste
- 1 cup chicken broth (or water)

Instructions:

Preheat Oven:
- Preheat your oven to 425°F (220°C).

Prepare Chicken:
- Pat the whole chicken dry with paper towels. Remove any giblets from the cavity if they are included.

Season Chicken:
- Season the chicken cavity with salt and pepper. Stuff the cavity with lemon halves, fresh rosemary sprigs, and smashed garlic cloves.

Tie Legs:
- If desired, tie the chicken legs together with kitchen twine to help the chicken cook evenly.

Rub with Olive Oil:
- Rub the outside of the chicken with olive oil. Season the entire chicken with salt and pepper.

Place in Roasting Pan:
- Place the seasoned chicken in a roasting pan, breast side up.

Roast:
- Roast the chicken in the preheated oven for about 15 minutes to allow the skin to crisp up.

Reduce Temperature:
- Reduce the oven temperature to 375°F (190°C) and continue roasting until the internal temperature reaches 165°F (74°C). This usually takes about 20 minutes per pound, but the cooking time can vary.

Baste:
- Baste the chicken with its juices every 30 minutes to keep it moist.

Rest:

- Once the chicken reaches the desired temperature, remove it from the oven, tent it with foil, and let it rest for about 15 minutes before carving.

Serve:
- Carve the roast chicken and serve with the pan juices.

Tips:

- Crispy Skin: To achieve extra crispy skin, you can pat the chicken dry and let it air-dry in the refrigerator for a few hours or overnight before roasting.
- Flavor Variations: Experiment with additional herbs and spices, such as thyme or paprika, to customize the flavor.

This roast chicken with lemon and rosemary is not only delicious but also a simple and elegant dish that's perfect for any occasion. Enjoy the juicy and flavorful results!

Baked Salmon with Dill Sauce

Baked Salmon:

Ingredients:

- 4 salmon fillets
- Salt and black pepper, to taste
- 2 tablespoons olive oil
- 2 tablespoons lemon juice
- 2 cloves garlic, minced
- 1 teaspoon dried or fresh dill, chopped
- Lemon slices, for garnish (optional)

Instructions:

Preheat Oven:
- Preheat your oven to 375°F (190°C).

Season Salmon:
- Pat the salmon fillets dry with paper towels. Season both sides with salt and black pepper.

Make Marinade:
- In a small bowl, mix together olive oil, lemon juice, minced garlic, and chopped dill.

Marinate Salmon:
- Place the salmon fillets in a baking dish. Pour the marinade over the salmon, ensuring they are well-coated. Let them marinate for about 15-20 minutes.

Bake:
- Bake the salmon in the preheated oven for 15-20 minutes or until the salmon flakes easily with a fork.

Garnish and Serve:
- Garnish with additional dill and lemon slices if desired. Serve the baked salmon with dill sauce.

Dill Sauce:

Ingredients:

- 1/2 cup Greek yogurt or sour cream
- 1 tablespoon fresh dill, chopped

- 1 teaspoon Dijon mustard
- 1 teaspoon honey (adjust to taste)
- Salt and black pepper, to taste

Instructions:

> Make Dill Sauce:
> - In a small bowl, mix together Greek yogurt or sour cream, chopped dill, Dijon mustard, honey, salt, and black pepper.
>
> Adjust Seasoning:
> - Taste the sauce and adjust the seasoning or sweetness according to your preference.
>
> Chill:
> - Refrigerate the dill sauce for at least 15 minutes to allow the flavors to meld.
>
> Serve:
> - Serve the baked salmon with a dollop of dill sauce on top or on the side.

Tips:

- Fresh Dill: If using fresh dill, adjust the quantity to your liking for a more pronounced flavor.
- Salmon Varieties: This recipe works well with various salmon varieties, such as Atlantic or sockeye.

This baked salmon with dill sauce is a simple and flavorful way to enjoy this nutritious fish. The dill sauce adds a zesty and herby kick to complement the richness of the salmon. Enjoy this dish for a healthy and satisfying meal!

Vegetarian Stuffed Peppers

Ingredients:

- 4 large bell peppers, halved and seeds removed
- 1 cup quinoa, cooked
- 1 can (15 oz) black beans, drained and rinsed
- 1 cup corn kernels (fresh or frozen)
- 1 cup diced tomatoes
- 1 cup shredded cheese (cheddar, Monterey Jack, or a blend)
- 1/2 cup diced red onion
- 2 cloves garlic, minced
- 1 teaspoon ground cumin
- 1 teaspoon chili powder
- Salt and black pepper, to taste
- Fresh cilantro or parsley for garnish (optional)

Instructions:

Preheat Oven:
- Preheat your oven to 375°F (190°C).

Prepare Peppers:
- Cut the bell peppers in half lengthwise, removing seeds and membranes. Place them in a baking dish.

Cook Quinoa:
- Cook quinoa according to package instructions. Fluff with a fork and set aside.

Prepare Filling:
- In a large bowl, combine cooked quinoa, black beans, corn, diced tomatoes, shredded cheese, red onion, minced garlic, ground cumin, chili powder, salt, and black pepper. Mix well.

Stuff Peppers:
- Spoon the quinoa mixture into each bell pepper half, pressing down gently to pack the filling.

Bake:
- Cover the baking dish with foil and bake in the preheated oven for 25-30 minutes, or until the peppers are tender.

Optional Broil:
- If you like a slightly crispy top, you can remove the foil and broil for an additional 3-5 minutes, watching closely to prevent burning.

Garnish and Serve:
- Garnish with fresh cilantro or parsley if desired. Serve the stuffed peppers hot.

Tips:

- Customize Fillings: Feel free to add ingredients like diced zucchini, olives, or jalapeños for extra flavor.
- Make-Ahead: You can prepare the filling in advance and stuff the peppers just before baking.

These vegetarian stuffed peppers are a nutritious and satisfying meal, providing a wonderful combination of flavors and textures. Enjoy this meatless dish as a main course for a healthy and hearty dinner!

Sides:

Scalloped Potatoes

Ingredients:

- 4 cups potatoes, peeled and thinly sliced (about 4-5 medium-sized potatoes)
- 1/4 cup unsalted butter
- 1/4 cup all-purpose flour
- 2 cups milk
- 1 cup heavy cream
- 2 cups shredded cheddar cheese
- 2 cloves garlic, minced
- Salt and black pepper, to taste
- 1/4 teaspoon ground nutmeg (optional)
- Fresh parsley, chopped, for garnish (optional)

Instructions:

Preheat Oven:
- Preheat your oven to 350°F (175°C).

Prepare Potatoes:
- Peel and thinly slice the potatoes, aiming for about 1/8-inch thickness.

Make Cheese Sauce:
- In a saucepan over medium heat, melt the butter. Add the minced garlic and sauté for about 1 minute until fragrant.
- Stir in the flour to create a roux. Cook for 2-3 minutes, stirring constantly.
- Gradually whisk in the milk and heavy cream, ensuring there are no lumps.
- Continue to cook and stir until the mixture thickens. Reduce heat to low and add the shredded cheddar cheese. Stir until the cheese is melted and the sauce is smooth. Season with salt, black pepper, and ground nutmeg (if using). Remove from heat.

Layer Potatoes:
- In a greased baking dish, layer half of the sliced potatoes. Pour half of the cheese sauce over the potatoes, ensuring an even coating.
- Repeat the layering with the remaining potatoes and cheese sauce.

Bake:
- Cover the baking dish with foil and bake in the preheated oven for about 40-50 minutes or until the potatoes are fork-tender.

Broil (Optional):
- If you like a golden top, you can remove the foil and broil for an additional 3-5 minutes, watching closely to prevent burning.

Garnish and Serve:
- Garnish with chopped fresh parsley if desired. Let it rest for a few minutes before serving.

Tips:

- Thin Slices: Ensure that the potato slices are thinly cut for even cooking.
- Cheese Variations: Feel free to experiment with different types of cheese, such as gruyere or Parmesan.

These creamy and cheesy scalloped potatoes make for a wonderful side dish that pairs well with a variety of main courses. Enjoy the rich and comforting flavors!

Glazed Carrots with Maple Syrup

Ingredients:

- 1 pound carrots, peeled and sliced into thin rounds or sticks
- 2 tablespoons unsalted butter
- 2 tablespoons pure maple syrup
- Salt and black pepper, to taste
- Fresh parsley, chopped, for garnish (optional)

Instructions:

Prepare Carrots:
- Peel and slice the carrots into thin rounds or sticks, whichever you prefer.

Steam or Boil Carrots:
- Steam or boil the carrots until they are just tender, about 5-7 minutes. Drain excess water.

Make Glaze:
- In a large skillet over medium heat, melt the butter. Add the maple syrup and stir to combine.

Add Carrots:
- Add the steamed or boiled carrots to the skillet, tossing to coat them evenly with the maple syrup glaze.

Sauté:
- Sauté the carrots in the glaze for an additional 2-3 minutes, or until they are fully coated and the glaze has thickened slightly.

Season:
- Season with salt and black pepper to taste. Adjust sweetness or add more maple syrup if desired.

Garnish and Serve:
- Transfer the glazed carrots to a serving dish. Garnish with chopped fresh parsley if desired.

Tips:

- Texture Preference: You can adjust the cooking time to achieve your preferred level of tenderness for the carrots.
- Variations: Enhance the flavor by adding a pinch of ground cinnamon or a sprinkle of toasted nuts.

These glazed carrots with maple syrup are a delightful combination of sweet and savory flavors, making them a perfect side dish for various meals. Enjoy!

Lemon Garlic Roasted Asparagus

Ingredients:

- 1 bunch of fresh asparagus, tough ends trimmed
- 2 tablespoons olive oil
- 3 cloves garlic, minced
- Zest of 1 lemon
- 2 tablespoons freshly squeezed lemon juice
- Salt and black pepper, to taste
- Parmesan cheese, grated (optional, for serving)
- Fresh parsley, chopped, for garnish (optional)

Instructions:

Preheat Oven:
- Preheat your oven to 400°F (200°C).

Prepare Asparagus:
- Trim the tough ends of the asparagus spears.

Season Asparagus:
- Place the asparagus on a baking sheet. Drizzle olive oil over the asparagus and toss to coat evenly. Spread the asparagus in a single layer on the baking sheet.

Add Garlic and Lemon:
- Sprinkle minced garlic, lemon zest, and lemon juice over the asparagus. Toss to combine, ensuring the asparagus is coated with the garlic and lemon.

Season with Salt and Pepper:
- Season the asparagus with salt and black pepper according to your taste.

Roast:
- Roast in the preheated oven for about 12-15 minutes or until the asparagus is tender but still has a slight crispness.

Garnish and Serve:
- Transfer the roasted asparagus to a serving platter. If desired, sprinkle with grated Parmesan cheese and chopped fresh parsley for added flavor.

Tips:

- Lemon Variations: Experiment with other citrus flavors like orange or lime for a different twist.

- Tender Asparagus: The cooking time may vary depending on the thickness of the asparagus. Thicker spears may require a few extra minutes.

This lemon garlic roasted asparagus is a bright and refreshing side dish that pairs well with a variety of main courses. Enjoy the vibrant flavors!

Creamy Spinach and Artichoke Casserole

Ingredients:

- 1 pound fresh spinach, washed and chopped
- 1 can (14 oz) artichoke hearts, drained and chopped
- 1 cup cream cheese, softened
- 1 cup sour cream
- 1 cup mayonnaise
- 1 cup shredded mozzarella cheese
- 1/2 cup grated Parmesan cheese
- 3 cloves garlic, minced
- 1 teaspoon onion powder
- Salt and black pepper, to taste
- 1/2 cup breadcrumbs (optional, for topping)
- Fresh parsley, chopped, for garnish (optional)

Instructions:

Preheat Oven:
- Preheat your oven to 350°F (175°C).

Sauté Spinach:
- In a large skillet, sauté the chopped spinach over medium heat until wilted. Drain any excess liquid.

Combine Ingredients:
- In a large mixing bowl, combine the cream cheese, sour cream, mayonnaise, shredded mozzarella, grated Parmesan, minced garlic, onion powder, salt, and black pepper. Mix until well combined.

Add Spinach and Artichokes:
- Stir in the sautéed spinach and chopped artichoke hearts into the cream cheese mixture. Mix thoroughly.

Transfer to Baking Dish:
- Transfer the mixture to a greased baking dish, spreading it evenly.

Optional Topping:
- If desired, sprinkle breadcrumbs over the top for a crispy texture.

Bake:
- Bake in the preheated oven for approximately 25-30 minutes, or until the casserole is hot and bubbly.

Garnish and Serve:

- Garnish with fresh chopped parsley if desired. Serve the creamy spinach and artichoke casserole hot.

Tips:

- Breadcrumbs Topping: If you choose to add breadcrumbs, consider mixing them with a bit of melted butter before sprinkling over the casserole for added richness.
- Make-Ahead: You can prepare the casserole ahead of time and refrigerate it until ready to bake.

This creamy spinach and artichoke casserole is a crowd-pleaser and makes for a delicious side dish or appetizer for gatherings. Enjoy the rich and flavorful combination of spinach and artichokes!

Wild Rice Pilaf with Mushrooms

Ingredients:

- 1 cup wild rice, rinsed
- 2 cups vegetable or chicken broth
- 1 tablespoon olive oil
- 1 onion, finely chopped
- 2 cloves garlic, minced
- 8 oz (about 227g) mushrooms, sliced (button mushrooms or a mix of wild mushrooms)
- 1 teaspoon fresh thyme leaves (or 1/2 teaspoon dried thyme)
- Salt and black pepper, to taste
- 1/4 cup chopped fresh parsley, for garnish (optional)

Instructions:

Cook Wild Rice:
- In a medium saucepan, combine the rinsed wild rice and broth. Bring to a boil, then reduce the heat to low, cover, and simmer for about 45-50 minutes or until the rice is tender and has absorbed most of the liquid. Drain any excess liquid if necessary.

Sauté Onion and Garlic:
- In a large skillet, heat olive oil over medium heat. Add the chopped onion and sauté until softened, about 3-4 minutes. Add minced garlic and cook for an additional 1 minute.

Add Mushrooms:
- Add the sliced mushrooms to the skillet. Cook until the mushrooms are browned and any released liquid has evaporated, about 5-7 minutes.

Combine Rice and Mushrooms:
- Add the cooked wild rice to the skillet with the mushrooms and onions. Stir to combine.

Season:
- Season the pilaf with fresh thyme, salt, and black pepper. Adjust the seasoning to taste.

Garnish and Serve:
- Garnish with chopped fresh parsley if desired. Serve the wild rice pilaf with mushrooms hot.

Tips:

- Wild Rice Mixture: You can mix wild rice with other rice varieties for added texture and flavor.
- Nut Variations: Consider adding toasted nuts, such as almonds or pecans, for an extra crunch.

This wild rice pilaf with mushrooms is a hearty and nutritious side dish that pairs well with a variety of main courses. Enjoy the earthy flavors of wild rice and mushrooms!

Salads:

Spring Mix Salad with Strawberries and Goat Cheese

Ingredients:

- 6 cups spring mix salad greens
- 1 pint strawberries, hulled and sliced
- 4 oz (about 113g) goat cheese, crumbled
- 1/4 cup sliced almonds, toasted
- Balsamic vinaigrette dressing
- Salt and black pepper, to taste

Instructions:

Prepare Salad Greens:
- Wash and dry the spring mix salad greens thoroughly. Place them in a large salad bowl.

Add Strawberries:
- Hull the strawberries and slice them. Add the sliced strawberries to the salad greens.

Crumble Goat Cheese:
- Crumble the goat cheese over the salad. You can either crumble it with your hands or use a fork.

Toast Almonds:
- In a dry skillet over medium heat, toast the sliced almonds until they are golden brown and fragrant. Keep a close eye on them, as they can burn quickly.

Sprinkle Toasted Almonds:
- Sprinkle the toasted almonds over the salad for added crunch.

Season:
- Season the salad with a pinch of salt and black pepper, to taste.

Dress the Salad:
- Drizzle the balsamic vinaigrette dressing over the salad. Toss gently to coat the ingredients evenly.

Serve:
- Serve the spring mix salad with strawberries and goat cheese immediately.

Tips:

- Dressing Variation: If you prefer a different dressing, consider using a honey mustard vinaigrette or a raspberry vinaigrette for a fruity twist.
- Additional Ingredients: You can add avocado slices, red onion rings, or fresh herbs like mint or basil for extra flavor.

This spring mix salad with strawberries and goat cheese is a perfect balance of sweet and savory flavors. Enjoy it as a light and vibrant side dish or add grilled chicken or shrimp to make it a complete meal!

Greek Salad with Feta and Kalamata Olives

Ingredients:

- 4 cups chopped Romaine lettuce or mixed salad greens
- 1 cup cherry tomatoes, halved
- 1 cucumber, diced
- 1 red bell pepper, diced
- 1/2 red onion, thinly sliced
- 1 cup Kalamata olives, pitted
- 1 cup feta cheese, crumbled
- 1/4 cup fresh parsley, chopped
- 1/4 cup extra virgin olive oil
- 2 tablespoons red wine vinegar
- 1 teaspoon dried oregano
- Salt and black pepper, to taste

Instructions:

Prepare Vegetables:
- Chop the Romaine lettuce or mixed salad greens and place them in a large salad bowl.

Add Vegetables:
- Add the halved cherry tomatoes, diced cucumber, diced red bell pepper, and thinly sliced red onion to the bowl.

Add Olives and Feta:
- Toss in the Kalamata olives and crumbled feta cheese.

Sprinkle Parsley:
- Sprinkle the chopped fresh parsley over the salad.

Prepare Dressing:
- In a small bowl, whisk together the extra virgin olive oil, red wine vinegar, dried oregano, salt, and black pepper. Adjust the seasoning to taste.

Dress the Salad:
- Drizzle the dressing over the salad. Toss gently to coat the ingredients evenly.

Serve:
- Serve the Greek salad with feta and Kalamata olives immediately.

Tips:

- Additional Ingredients: You can customize the salad by adding ingredients like sliced black olives, capers, or pepperoncini for extra flavor.
- Protein Addition: For a heartier meal, consider adding grilled chicken, shrimp, or chickpeas.

This Greek salad with feta and Kalamata olives is a refreshing and satisfying dish that captures the essence of Mediterranean flavors. Enjoy it as a light lunch or a flavorful side dish!

Roasted Beet and Arugula Salad

Ingredients:

- 4 medium-sized beets, peeled and cubed
- 2 tablespoons olive oil
- Salt and black pepper, to taste
- 6 cups arugula, washed and dried
- 1/2 cup crumbled goat cheese
- 1/4 cup balsamic vinaigrette dressing
- 1/4 cup toasted walnuts or pecans, chopped
- Fresh basil or mint leaves, for garnish (optional)

Instructions:

Roast Beets:
- Preheat your oven to 400°F (200°C).
- Place the cubed beets on a baking sheet. Drizzle with olive oil and season with salt and black pepper. Toss to coat evenly.
- Roast in the preheated oven for about 25-30 minutes or until the beets are tender. Allow them to cool slightly.

Assemble Salad:
- In a large salad bowl, combine the arugula, roasted beets, and crumbled goat cheese.

Dress Salad:
- Drizzle the balsamic vinaigrette dressing over the salad. Toss gently to combine.

Add Nuts:
- Sprinkle the chopped toasted walnuts or pecans over the salad for added crunch.

Garnish:
- If desired, garnish with fresh basil or mint leaves for a burst of freshness.

Serve:
- Serve the roasted beet and arugula salad immediately.

Tips:

- Goat Cheese Variation: You can use feta or blue cheese as alternatives to goat cheese.
- Citrus Dressing: Consider a citrus-based dressing for a tangy twist.

This roasted beet and arugula salad is not only visually appealing but also a delightful combination of earthy and peppery flavors. Enjoy it as a light and nutritious meal or as a side dish to complement your main course!

Citrus Avocado Salad

Ingredients:

- 4 cups mixed salad greens (e.g., spinach, arugula, and/or watercress)
- 2 ripe avocados, peeled, pitted, and sliced
- 1 grapefruit, segmented
- 2 oranges, segmented
- 1/4 cup red onion, thinly sliced
- 1/4 cup fresh mint leaves, chopped
- 1/4 cup extra virgin olive oil
- 2 tablespoons fresh lime juice
- Salt and black pepper, to taste
- 1/4 cup chopped nuts (e.g., pistachios or almonds), toasted (optional)

Instructions:

Prepare Salad Greens:
- Wash and dry the mixed salad greens. Place them in a large salad bowl.

Add Avocados and Citrus Segments:
- Add the sliced avocados, grapefruit segments, and orange segments to the salad greens.

Add Red Onion and Mint:
- Sprinkle the thinly sliced red onion and chopped fresh mint leaves over the salad.

Prepare Dressing:
- In a small bowl, whisk together the extra virgin olive oil and fresh lime juice. Season with salt and black pepper to taste.

Dress the Salad:
- Drizzle the dressing over the salad. Gently toss to coat the ingredients evenly.

Optional Toasted Nuts:
- If desired, sprinkle the toasted nuts over the salad for added texture.

Serve:
- Serve the citrus avocado salad immediately.

Tips:

- Variety of Citrus: Experiment with different citrus fruits like mandarins or blood oranges for unique flavors.

- Protein Addition: Consider adding grilled chicken, shrimp, or chickpeas for a protein boost.

This citrus avocado salad is a vibrant and flavorful option for a light lunch or a refreshing side dish. Enjoy the combination of creamy avocado and bright citrus flavors!

Broccoli Salad with Bacon and Cranberries

Ingredients:

- 4 cups broccoli florets, chopped into bite-sized pieces
- 1/2 cup red onion, finely chopped
- 1/2 cup dried cranberries
- 1/2 cup crispy bacon, crumbled
- 1/2 cup sunflower seeds
- 1/2 cup mayonnaise
- 2 tablespoons apple cider vinegar
- 2 tablespoons honey
- Salt and black pepper, to taste

Instructions:

Prepare Broccoli:
- Wash and chop the broccoli into bite-sized florets.

Combine Ingredients:
- In a large mixing bowl, combine the chopped broccoli, finely chopped red onion, dried cranberries, crumbled bacon, and sunflower seeds.

Make Dressing:
- In a small bowl, whisk together the mayonnaise, apple cider vinegar, honey, salt, and black pepper.

Dress the Salad:
- Pour the dressing over the broccoli mixture. Toss gently to coat the ingredients evenly with the dressing.

Chill:
- Cover the salad and refrigerate for at least 1 hour before serving. This allows the flavors to meld.

Serve:
- Before serving, give the salad a final toss. Adjust the seasoning if needed. Serve the broccoli salad chilled.

Tips:

- Make-Ahead: This salad can be prepared a few hours in advance, making it a convenient option for gatherings.
- Cheese Addition: Consider adding crumbled feta or shredded cheddar cheese for an extra layer of flavor.

This broccoli salad with bacon and cranberries is a crowd-pleaser with its combination of crunchy broccoli, savory bacon, and sweet cranberries. Enjoy it as a side dish for barbecues, picnics, or any meal!

Breads:

Hot Cross Buns

Ingredients:

For the Buns:

- 4 cups all-purpose flour
- 1/2 cup sugar
- 1 packet (2 1/4 teaspoons) active dry yeast
- 1 1/2 teaspoons ground cinnamon
- 1/2 teaspoon ground nutmeg
- 1/2 teaspoon salt
- 1 1/4 cups milk, warmed
- 1/4 cup unsalted butter, melted
- 1 large egg
- 1 cup currants or raisins

For the Cross:

- 1/2 cup all-purpose flour
- 1/2 cup water

For the Glaze:

- 1/4 cup apricot preserves or orange marmalade (for a shiny finish)

Instructions:

Prepare Dough:
- In a large bowl, combine 4 cups of flour, sugar, yeast, cinnamon, nutmeg, and salt.

Warm Milk and Melt Butter:
- In a separate bowl, warm the milk (about 110°F or 43°C) and melt the butter.

Combine Wet Ingredients:
- Whisk together the warm milk, melted butter, and the egg.

Make Dough:
- Add the wet ingredients to the dry ingredients, and mix until a soft dough forms. Add more flour if needed.

Knead and Add Currants:
- Turn the dough onto a floured surface and knead for about 8-10 minutes until smooth and elastic. Incorporate the currants or raisins during the last few minutes of kneading.

First Rise:
- Place the dough in a greased bowl, cover it with a damp cloth, and let it rise in a warm place for about 1 hour or until it doubles in size.

Shape Buns:
- Punch down the dough, divide it into 12 equal portions, and shape each into a round bun. Place them in a greased baking pan.

Prepare Cross Mixture:
- In a small bowl, mix 1/2 cup flour with 1/2 cup water to form a thick paste. Pipe a cross onto each bun using this mixture.

Second Rise:
- Cover the buns with a damp cloth and let them rise for another 30 minutes.

Preheat Oven:
- Preheat your oven to 375°F (190°C).

Bake:
- Bake the buns for 15-20 minutes or until golden brown.

Make Glaze:
- While the buns are baking, heat the apricot preserves or orange marmalade in a small saucepan until melted.

Glaze Buns:
- Brush the warm buns with the melted preserves or marmalade for a shiny finish.

Cool and Serve:
- Allow the hot cross buns to cool before serving.

Tips:

- Variations: You can customize the spicing and add citrus zest for extra flavor.
- Icing Crosses: If you prefer an icing cross, you can make a simple glaze using powdered sugar and milk.

Enjoy these hot cross buns as a festive treat during the Easter season!

Easter Braided Bread

Ingredients:

For the Dough:

- 4 to 4 1/2 cups all-purpose flour
- 1/2 cup sugar
- 1 packet (2 1/4 teaspoons) active dry yeast
- 1 teaspoon salt
- 1 teaspoon ground cardamom (optional)
- 1/2 cup unsalted butter, melted
- 1 cup warm milk
- 3 large eggs

For the Egg Wash:

- 1 egg, beaten
- 1 tablespoon milk

For Decoration (Optional):

- Colored sprinkles or sesame seeds

Instructions:

Activate Yeast:
- In a small bowl, combine warm milk and a pinch of sugar. Sprinkle the yeast over the milk and let it sit for about 5-10 minutes until it becomes frothy.

Combine Dry Ingredients:
- In a large bowl, whisk together 4 cups of flour, sugar, salt, and cardamom (if using).

Make Dough:
- Create a well in the center of the dry ingredients. Pour in the activated yeast mixture, melted butter, and eggs. Mix until a soft dough forms.

Knead Dough:
- Turn the dough onto a floured surface and knead for about 10-12 minutes until it becomes smooth and elastic. Add more flour if needed.

First Rise:
- Place the dough in a greased bowl, cover it with a damp cloth, and let it rise in a warm place for about 1-2 hours or until it doubles in size.

Punch Down and Braid:
- Punch down the dough and divide it into three equal portions. Roll each portion into a long rope. Braid the ropes together and form a braided loaf.

Second Rise:
- Place the braided loaf on a baking sheet lined with parchment paper. Cover it with a damp cloth and let it rise for another 1-2 hours.

Preheat Oven:
- Preheat your oven to 350°F (180°C).

Egg Wash:
- In a small bowl, mix the beaten egg with 1 tablespoon of milk. Brush the egg wash over the braided loaf.

Decoration (Optional):
- If desired, sprinkle colored sprinkles or sesame seeds over the egg wash.

Bake:
- Bake in the preheated oven for 25-30 minutes or until the bread is golden brown and sounds hollow when tapped on the bottom.

Cool:
- Allow the Easter braided bread to cool on a wire rack before slicing.

Tips:

- Flavor Variations: You can add citrus zest, vanilla extract, or a hint of ground nutmeg for additional flavor.
- Bread Glaze: After baking, you can brush the bread with a simple sugar glaze made with powdered sugar and a little milk for added sweetness.

Enjoy this Easter braided bread as a centerpiece for your Easter table or as a delightful treat during the holiday season!

Garlic and Herb Dinner Rolls

Ingredients:

For the Dough:

- 4 to 4 1/2 cups all-purpose flour
- 1/4 cup sugar
- 1 packet (2 1/4 teaspoons) active dry yeast
- 1 teaspoon salt
- 1 cup warm milk (about 110°F or 43°C)
- 1/4 cup unsalted butter, melted
- 2 large eggs

For the Garlic and Herb Butter:

- 1/2 cup unsalted butter, softened
- 3 cloves garlic, minced
- 1 tablespoon fresh parsley, finely chopped
- 1 teaspoon dried oregano
- 1 teaspoon dried thyme
- 1/2 teaspoon salt

Instructions:

For the Dough:

Activate Yeast:
- In a small bowl, combine warm milk and a pinch of sugar. Sprinkle the yeast over the milk and let it sit for about 5-10 minutes until it becomes frothy.

Combine Dry Ingredients:
- In a large bowl, whisk together 4 cups of flour, sugar, and salt.

Make Dough:
- Create a well in the center of the dry ingredients. Pour in the activated yeast mixture, melted butter, and eggs. Mix until a soft dough forms.

Knead Dough:
- Turn the dough onto a floured surface and knead for about 8-10 minutes until it becomes smooth and elastic. Add more flour if needed.

First Rise:
- Place the dough in a greased bowl, cover it with a damp cloth, and let it rise in a warm place for about 1 hour or until it doubles in size.

For the Garlic and Herb Butter:

Prepare Garlic Herb Butter:
- In a small bowl, mix together softened butter, minced garlic, chopped fresh parsley, dried oregano, dried thyme, and salt. Set aside.

Assembling and Baking:

Preheat Oven:
- Preheat your oven to 375°F (190°C).

Divide Dough:
- Punch down the risen dough and divide it into equal portions to form individual rolls.

Shape Rolls:
- Shape each portion into a ball and place them in a greased baking pan, leaving a small gap between each roll.

Spread Garlic Herb Butter:
- Spread a generous amount of the prepared garlic and herb butter over the top of each roll.

Second Rise:
- Cover the rolls with a damp cloth and let them rise for another 20-30 minutes.

Bake:
- Bake in the preheated oven for 15-20 minutes or until the rolls are golden brown.

Serve:
- Serve the garlic and herb dinner rolls warm.

Tips:
- **Fresh Herbs:** If you have fresh herbs on hand, feel free to use them instead of dried ones for an extra burst of flavor.
- **Cheese Addition:** Consider adding grated Parmesan or shredded mozzarella to the garlic herb butter for cheesy dinner rolls.

These garlic and herb dinner rolls will fill your kitchen with a wonderful aroma and complement a variety of dishes. Enjoy them as a side for dinner or on their own as a tasty snack!

Spinach and Feta Stuffed Bread

Ingredients:

For the Dough:

- 4 cups all-purpose flour
- 1 tablespoon sugar
- 1 packet (2 1/4 teaspoons) active dry yeast
- 1 teaspoon salt
- 1 cup warm water (about 110°F or 43°C)
- 2 tablespoons olive oil

For the Filling:

- 1 tablespoon olive oil
- 2 cloves garlic, minced
- 1 (10-ounce) package frozen chopped spinach, thawed and squeezed dry
- 1 cup crumbled feta cheese
- Salt and black pepper, to taste

For Topping:

- 1 egg, beaten (for egg wash)
- Sesame seeds or poppy seeds (optional)

Instructions:

For the Dough:

Activate Yeast:
- In a small bowl, combine warm water and sugar. Sprinkle the yeast over the water and let it sit for about 5-10 minutes until it becomes frothy.

Combine Dry Ingredients:
- In a large bowl, whisk together 4 cups of flour and salt.

Make Dough:
- Create a well in the center of the dry ingredients. Pour in the activated yeast mixture and olive oil. Mix until a soft dough forms.

Knead Dough:
- Turn the dough onto a floured surface and knead for about 8-10 minutes until it becomes smooth and elastic. Add more flour if needed.

First Rise:

- Place the dough in a greased bowl, cover it with a damp cloth, and let it rise in a warm place for about 1 hour or until it doubles in size.

For the Filling:

Prepare Filling:
- In a skillet, heat 1 tablespoon of olive oil over medium heat. Add minced garlic and sauté for about 1 minute until fragrant.

Add Spinach:
- Add the thawed and squeezed dry spinach to the skillet. Cook for a few minutes until any excess moisture evaporates.

Combine with Feta:
- Remove the skillet from heat and stir in the crumbled feta. Season with salt and black pepper to taste. Allow the mixture to cool.

Assembling and Baking:

Preheat Oven:
- Preheat your oven to 375°F (190°C).

Roll Out Dough:
- On a floured surface, roll out the risen dough into a rectangle.

Add Filling:
- Spread the cooled spinach and feta mixture evenly over the rolled-out dough.

Roll and Seal:
- Starting from one of the longer edges, roll the dough into a log. Seal the edges by pinching them together.

Place on Baking Sheet:
- Place the rolled log on a baking sheet lined with parchment paper.

Second Rise:
- Cover the stuffed bread with a damp cloth and let it rise for another 20-30 minutes.

Brush with Egg Wash:
- Brush the surface of the stuffed bread with the beaten egg. Optionally, sprinkle sesame seeds or poppy seeds over the top.

Bake:
- Bake in the preheated oven for 25-30 minutes or until the bread is golden brown.

Cool and Slice:
- Allow the spinach and feta stuffed bread to cool slightly before slicing.

Tips:

- Add Sun-Dried Tomatoes: For an extra burst of flavor, consider adding chopped sun-dried tomatoes to the spinach and feta mixture.
- Serve with Dip: Serve the sliced stuffed bread with tzatziki or your favorite dipping sauce.

This spinach and feta stuffed bread is a savory and satisfying treat. Enjoy it warm, and share it with friends and family!

Carrot and Walnut Bread

Ingredients:

- 2 cups all-purpose flour
- 1 teaspoon baking powder
- 1/2 teaspoon baking soda
- 1/2 teaspoon salt
- 1 teaspoon ground cinnamon
- 1/2 teaspoon ground nutmeg
- 1/2 cup unsalted butter, melted
- 1/2 cup granulated sugar
- 1/2 cup brown sugar, packed
- 2 large eggs
- 1 teaspoon vanilla extract
- 1 1/2 cups grated carrots (about 3 medium-sized carrots)
- 1/2 cup chopped walnuts

Instructions:

Preheat Oven:
- Preheat your oven to 350°F (175°C). Grease and flour a 9x5-inch loaf pan.

Mix Dry Ingredients:
- In a medium-sized bowl, whisk together the flour, baking powder, baking soda, salt, cinnamon, and nutmeg. Set aside.

Combine Wet Ingredients:
- In a large bowl, whisk together the melted butter, granulated sugar, brown sugar, eggs, and vanilla extract until well combined.

Add Grated Carrots:
- Fold in the grated carrots into the wet ingredients.

Incorporate Dry Ingredients:
- Gradually add the dry ingredients to the wet ingredients, stirring until just combined. Do not overmix.

Add Chopped Walnuts:
- Gently fold in the chopped walnuts into the batter.

Fill the Loaf Pan:
- Pour the batter into the prepared loaf pan, spreading it evenly.

Bake:
- Bake in the preheated oven for 50-60 minutes or until a toothpick inserted into the center comes out clean or with a few moist crumbs.

Cool:
- Allow the carrot and walnut bread to cool in the pan for about 10 minutes, then transfer it to a wire rack to cool completely.

Slice and Serve:
- Once cooled, slice the bread and serve.

Tips:

- Add Raisins or Dried Cranberries: Consider adding a handful of raisins or dried cranberries for an extra burst of sweetness.
- Cream Cheese Frosting: If you want to make it more dessert-like, you can spread a thin layer of cream cheese frosting on top once the bread has cooled.

Enjoy this carrot and walnut bread with a cup of tea or coffee for a delightful treat!

Desserts:

Easter Bunny Sugar Cookies

Ingredients:

For the Sugar Cookies:

- 2 3/4 cups all-purpose flour
- 1 teaspoon baking soda
- 1/2 teaspoon baking powder
- 1 cup unsalted butter, softened
- 1 1/2 cups granulated sugar
- 1 large egg
- 1 teaspoon vanilla extract

For Royal Icing:

- 2 cups powdered sugar
- 1 large egg white
- 1/2 teaspoon vanilla extract
- Food coloring (optional)

Instructions:

For the Sugar Cookies:

> Preheat Oven:
> - Preheat your oven to 375°F (190°C). Line baking sheets with parchment paper.
>
> Mix Dry Ingredients:
> - In a medium bowl, whisk together the flour, baking soda, and baking powder. Set aside.
>
> Cream Butter and Sugar:
> - In a large bowl, cream together the softened butter and granulated sugar until light and fluffy.
>
> Add Egg and Vanilla:
> - Beat in the egg and vanilla extract until well combined.
>
> Incorporate Dry Ingredients:

- Gradually add the dry ingredients to the wet ingredients, mixing until just combined.

Chill Dough:
- Divide the dough into two portions, shape each into a disc, wrap in plastic wrap, and refrigerate for at least 1 hour.

Roll and Cut Shapes:
- Preheat your oven again to 375°F (190°C). On a floured surface, roll out the chilled dough to about 1/4 inch thickness. Cut out bunny shapes with cookie cutters.

Bake:
- Place the cut-out cookies on prepared baking sheets. Bake for 8-10 minutes or until the edges are lightly golden. Allow the cookies to cool completely.

For Royal Icing:

Prepare Icing:
- In a bowl, whisk together powdered sugar, egg white, and vanilla extract until smooth. Adjust the consistency by adding more powdered sugar if it's too thin or a little water if it's too thick.

Color Icing (Optional):
- Divide the icing into smaller bowls and add food coloring if you want to create different colors.

Decorate Cookies:
- Once the cookies are completely cool, use the royal icing to decorate the Easter bunny sugar cookies. You can outline and flood the cookies with different colors, and use additional icing or candies for details.

Let Icing Set:
- Allow the icing to set completely before storing or serving.

Tips:

- Use Piping Bags: To create intricate designs on the cookies, use piping bags for better control.
- Edible Decorations: Add edible decorations like sprinkles or edible glitter for extra festive flair.

Enjoy creating these Easter bunny sugar cookies as a fun and tasty addition to your holiday celebrations!

Carrot Cake with Cream Cheese Frosting

Ingredients:

For the Carrot Cake:

- 2 cups all-purpose flour
- 2 cups granulated sugar
- 1 teaspoon baking powder
- 1/2 teaspoon baking soda
- 1/2 teaspoon salt
- 1 teaspoon ground cinnamon
- 1/2 teaspoon ground nutmeg
- 1/2 cup vegetable oil
- 4 large eggs
- 1 teaspoon vanilla extract
- 2 cups grated carrots (about 3 medium-sized carrots)
- 1/2 cup crushed pineapple, drained
- 1/2 cup shredded coconut (optional)
- 1/2 cup chopped nuts (walnuts or pecans), optional

For the Cream Cheese Frosting:

- 8 ounces cream cheese, softened
- 1/2 cup unsalted butter, softened
- 4 cups powdered sugar
- 1 teaspoon vanilla extract

Instructions:

For the Carrot Cake:

Preheat Oven:
- Preheat your oven to 350°F (175°C). Grease and flour two 9-inch round cake pans.

Mix Dry Ingredients:
- In a large bowl, whisk together the flour, sugar, baking powder, baking soda, salt, cinnamon, and nutmeg.

Add Wet Ingredients:
- Add the vegetable oil, eggs, and vanilla extract to the dry ingredients. Mix until well combined.

Incorporate Carrots and Pineapple:

- Fold in the grated carrots, crushed pineapple, shredded coconut (if using), and chopped nuts (if using) until evenly distributed.

Divide Batter:
- Divide the batter equally between the prepared cake pans.

Bake:
- Bake in the preheated oven for 25-30 minutes or until a toothpick inserted into the center comes out clean.

Cool:
- Allow the cakes to cool in the pans for 10 minutes, then transfer them to a wire rack to cool completely.

For the Cream Cheese Frosting:

Beat Cream Cheese and Butter:
- In a large bowl, beat the softened cream cheese and butter until smooth and creamy.

Add Powdered Sugar and Vanilla:
- Gradually add the powdered sugar, beating continuously, until the frosting is smooth. Add the vanilla extract and mix until well combined.

Assemble the Cake:
- Once the cakes are completely cooled, spread a layer of cream cheese frosting on top of one cake layer. Place the second cake layer on top and frost the entire cake with the remaining cream cheese frosting.

Decorate (Optional):
- Optionally, you can decorate the cake with additional chopped nuts, shredded coconut, or carrot decorations.

Slice and Serve:
- Slice and serve the carrot cake, and enjoy!

Tips:

- Room Temperature Ingredients: Ensure that the cream cheese and butter for the frosting are at room temperature for a smooth consistency.
- Store in the Refrigerator: Due to the cream cheese frosting, store the finished cake in the refrigerator.

This carrot cake with cream cheese frosting is sure to be a crowd-pleaser, combining the sweetness of carrots with the rich and tangy creaminess of the frosting. Enjoy!

Lemon Tart with Raspberry Sauce

Ingredients:

For the Tart Crust:

- 1 1/2 cups all-purpose flour
- 1/2 cup powdered sugar
- 1/4 teaspoon salt
- 1/2 cup unsalted butter, cold and cut into small pieces
- 1 large egg yolk
- 1-2 tablespoons ice water

For the Lemon Filling:

- 4 large eggs
- 1 cup granulated sugar
- 1 cup fresh lemon juice (about 4-5 lemons)
- 1 tablespoon lemon zest
- 1/2 cup unsalted butter, melted and cooled

For the Raspberry Sauce:

- 1 cup fresh or frozen raspberries
- 2 tablespoons granulated sugar
- 1 tablespoon water
- 1 teaspoon lemon juice

Additional Garnish (Optional):

- Fresh raspberries
- Mint leaves

Instructions:

For the Tart Crust:

  Prepare Crust:
  - In a food processor, combine flour, powdered sugar, and salt. Add cold butter and pulse until the mixture resembles coarse crumbs.

  Add Egg Yolk:

- Add the egg yolk and pulse until the dough comes together. If needed, add ice water, one tablespoon at a time, until the dough forms a ball.

Chill Dough:
- Flatten the dough into a disk, wrap in plastic wrap, and refrigerate for at least 30 minutes.

Roll and Place in Tart Pan:
- Preheat your oven to 375°F (190°C). On a floured surface, roll out the chilled dough and press it into a tart pan. Trim any excess dough.

Blind Bake:
- Line the tart shell with parchment paper and fill it with pie weights or dried beans. Blind bake for 15 minutes. Remove the weights and parchment paper, then bake for an additional 10 minutes or until golden brown. Allow to cool.

For the Lemon Filling:

Prepare Filling:
- In a bowl, whisk together eggs, sugar, lemon juice, lemon zest, and melted butter until well combined.

Bake:
- Pour the lemon filling into the pre-baked tart shell. Bake for 15-20 minutes or until the filling is set.

Cool:
- Allow the tart to cool completely before refrigerating for at least 2 hours.

For the Raspberry Sauce:

Prepare Sauce:
- In a small saucepan, combine raspberries, sugar, water, and lemon juice. Cook over medium heat, stirring occasionally, until the raspberries break down and the sauce thickens.

Strain:
- Strain the sauce through a fine-mesh sieve to remove seeds. Allow it to cool.

Assemble and Serve:

Drizzle with Raspberry Sauce:
- Drizzle the cooled raspberry sauce over the chilled lemon tart.

Garnish (Optional):
- Garnish with fresh raspberries and mint leaves.

Slice and Serve:
- Slice the lemon tart and serve chilled. Enjoy!

This Lemon Tart with Raspberry Sauce is a delightful combination of sweet and tart flavors, making it a perfect dessert for any occasion.

Chocolate Nest Cupcakes

Ingredients:

For the Cupcakes:

- 1 1/2 cups all-purpose flour
- 1/2 cup unsweetened cocoa powder
- 1 teaspoon baking powder
- 1/2 teaspoon baking soda
- 1/4 teaspoon salt
- 1/2 cup unsalted butter, softened
- 1 cup granulated sugar
- 2 large eggs
- 1 teaspoon vanilla extract
- 1 cup buttermilk

For the Chocolate Frosting:

- 1 cup unsalted butter, softened
- 2 cups powdered sugar
- 1/2 cup unsweetened cocoa powder
- 1/4 cup milk
- 1 teaspoon vanilla extract

For the Chocolate Nests:

- 1 cup chocolate chips (dark or milk chocolate)
- 2 cups chow mein noodles

Additional Decoration:

- Mini chocolate eggs or candy-coated chocolate eggs

Instructions:

For the Cupcakes:

Preheat Oven:
- Preheat your oven to 350°F (175°C). Line a cupcake tin with paper liners.

Mix Dry Ingredients:
- In a bowl, whisk together flour, cocoa powder, baking powder, baking soda, and salt. Set aside.

Cream Butter and Sugar:
- In a large bowl, cream together the softened butter and granulated sugar until light and fluffy.

Add Eggs and Vanilla:
- Beat in the eggs one at a time, then add the vanilla extract.

Alternate Mixing:
- Gradually add the dry ingredients to the wet ingredients, alternating with buttermilk. Begin and end with the dry ingredients, mixing until just combined.

Fill Cupcake Liners:
- Divide the batter evenly among the cupcake liners, filling each about 2/3 full.

Bake:
- Bake in the preheated oven for 18-20 minutes or until a toothpick inserted into the center comes out clean. Allow cupcakes to cool completely.

For the Chocolate Frosting:

Cream Butter:
- In a large bowl, cream the softened butter until smooth.

Add Dry Ingredients:
- Gradually add powdered sugar and cocoa powder, mixing until well combined.

Pour Milk and Add Vanilla:
- Pour in the milk and add the vanilla extract. Beat until light and fluffy.

Frost Cupcakes:
- Frost the cooled cupcakes with the chocolate frosting using a piping bag or a spatula.

For the Chocolate Nests:

Melt Chocolate:
- In a microwave-safe bowl, melt the chocolate chips in 20-second intervals, stirring until smooth.

Add Chow Mein Noodles:
- Add the chow mein noodles to the melted chocolate and gently fold until well coated.

Form Nests:
- Spoon the chocolate and noodle mixture onto a parchment-lined tray, forming nest shapes. Create a well in the center of each nest.

Chill:
- Place the tray in the refrigerator to allow the chocolate nests to set.

Assemble and Decorate:

Place Nests on Cupcakes:
- Once the chocolate nests are set, carefully place one nest on top of each cupcake.

Add Mini Eggs:
- Place mini chocolate eggs or candy-coated chocolate eggs in the center of each nest.

Serve:
- Serve and enjoy your Chocolate Nest Cupcakes!

These adorable Chocolate Nest Cupcakes are not only delicious but also make a charming addition to your dessert table. Enjoy sharing them with family and friends!

Coconut Cream Pie

Ingredients:

For the Pie Crust:

- 1 1/4 cups all-purpose flour
- 1/2 cup unsalted butter, chilled and cut into small pieces
- 1/4 teaspoon salt
- 2-3 tablespoons ice water

For the Coconut Filling:

- 1 cup sweetened shredded coconut
- 2 cups whole milk
- 1 cup heavy cream
- 3/4 cup granulated sugar
- 1/2 cup cornstarch
- 1/4 teaspoon salt
- 4 large egg yolks, beaten
- 2 tablespoons unsalted butter
- 1 teaspoon vanilla extract

For Topping:

- 1 cup whipped cream
- Toasted coconut for garnish (optional)

Instructions:

For the Pie Crust:

  Prepare Crust:
  - In a food processor, combine the flour, butter, and salt. Pulse until the mixture resembles coarse crumbs.

  Add Water:
  - Add ice water, one tablespoon at a time, and pulse until the dough comes together.

  Form Dough:
  - Turn the dough out onto a floured surface and shape it into a disk. Wrap in plastic wrap and refrigerate for at least 1 hour.

Roll Out and Bake:
- Preheat your oven to 375°F (190°C). Roll out the chilled dough and fit it into a 9-inch pie dish. Trim and crimp the edges. Prick the bottom with a fork, line with parchment paper, and fill with pie weights or dried beans.

Blind Bake:
- Bake the crust for 15 minutes. Remove the parchment paper and weights, then bake for an additional 10-15 minutes or until golden brown. Allow to cool completely.

For the Coconut Filling:

Toast Coconut:
- In a dry skillet over medium heat, toast the shredded coconut until golden brown. Set aside for garnish.

Prepare Custard:
- In a saucepan, combine the milk, heavy cream, sugar, cornstarch, and salt. Cook over medium heat, stirring constantly, until the mixture thickens and comes to a boil.

Temper Eggs:
- Gradually whisk a small amount of the hot mixture into the beaten egg yolks to temper them. Then, whisk the egg yolk mixture back into the saucepan.

Cook and Remove from Heat:
- Cook, stirring constantly, for an additional 2 minutes until thickened. Remove from heat.

Add Coconut and Butter:
- Stir in the toasted coconut, butter, and vanilla extract until well combined.

Cool:
- Allow the coconut filling to cool for a few minutes, then pour it into the pre-baked pie crust. Refrigerate until set, at least 4 hours or overnight.

For Topping:

Whip Cream:
- Whip the cream until stiff peaks form.

Top and Garnish:
- Spread the whipped cream over the chilled coconut pie. Optionally, garnish with additional toasted coconut.

Serve:
- Slice and serve your delicious Coconut Cream Pie.

Enjoy this classic Coconut Cream Pie with its rich and creamy coconut filling!

Easter Egg Treats:

Chocolate Peanut Butter Eggs

Ingredients:

For the Peanut Butter Filling:

- 1 cup creamy peanut butter
- 1/4 cup unsalted butter, softened
- 2 cups powdered sugar
- 1 teaspoon vanilla extract

For the Chocolate Coating:

- 2 cups semi-sweet chocolate chips
- 2 tablespoons vegetable shortening or coconut oil

Instructions:

For the Peanut Butter Filling:

- Mix Peanut Butter Mixture:
  - In a bowl, combine creamy peanut butter, softened butter, powdered sugar, and vanilla extract. Mix until well combined and a dough-like consistency forms.
- Shape into Eggs:
  - Take a small portion of the peanut butter mixture and shape it into an egg form. Place the shaped eggs on a parchment-lined tray or plate.
- Chill:
  - Place the shaped peanut butter eggs in the refrigerator for at least 30 minutes to firm up.

For the Chocolate Coating:

- Melt Chocolate:
  - In a heatproof bowl, melt the chocolate chips and vegetable shortening or coconut oil together. You can melt them in the microwave in short intervals or use a double boiler on the stove.
- Coat Peanut Butter Eggs:

- Using a fork or toothpick, dip each chilled peanut butter egg into the melted chocolate, making sure it's fully coated. Allow excess chocolate to drip off.

Place on Parchment:
- Place the coated eggs back on the parchment-lined tray.

Chill Again:
- Put the tray back in the refrigerator to allow the chocolate coating to set. This will take about 1-2 hours.

Optional: Decorate (Optional):
- If desired, you can melt a small amount of white chocolate and drizzle it over the chocolate-coated peanut butter eggs for decoration.

Store:
- Once the chocolate coating is fully set, transfer the Chocolate Peanut Butter Eggs to an airtight container and store them in the refrigerator.

Tips:

- Customize: Feel free to customize the filling by adding chopped nuts or crispy rice cereal for added texture.
- Use Cookie Cutters: If you want specific shapes, you can also use cookie cutters to shape the peanut butter mixture.

These homemade Chocolate Peanut Butter Eggs are a delightful treat, especially during Easter or any time you're craving the classic combination of chocolate and peanut butter. Enjoy!

Marbled Easter Egg Truffles

Ingredients:

For the Truffle Base:

- 8 ounces cream cheese, softened
- 3 cups powdered sugar
- 1 teaspoon vanilla extract
- Pinch of salt

For the Marbled Coating:

- 12 ounces white chocolate, chopped
- Gel food coloring (assorted colors)

For Decorating:

- Edible luster dust or edible glitter (optional)
- Colored sprinkles or decorations (optional)

Instructions:

For the Truffle Base:

> Prepare Truffle Mixture:
> - In a large bowl, beat the softened cream cheese until smooth.
>
> Add Ingredients:
> - Gradually add the powdered sugar, vanilla extract, and a pinch of salt. Mix until well combined and a soft dough forms.
>
> Chill:
> - Cover the bowl and refrigerate the truffle mixture for at least 1 hour, or until it's firm enough to handle.
>
> Shape Eggs:
> - Take a small portion of the truffle mixture and shape it into egg forms. Place the shaped truffles on a parchment-lined tray and return them to the refrigerator while you prepare the marbled coating.

For the Marbled Coating:

> Melt White Chocolate:

- In a heatproof bowl, melt the white chocolate in the microwave or using a double boiler until smooth.

Divide and Color:
- Divide the melted white chocolate into separate bowls for each color you want to use. Add a small amount of gel food coloring to each bowl and swirl gently to create a marbled effect.

Dip and Coat:
- Using a fork or toothpick, dip each chilled truffle into the colored white chocolate, making sure to coat it completely. Allow excess chocolate to drip off.

Place on Tray:
- Place the coated truffles back on the parchment-lined tray.

Decorate (Optional):
- While the chocolate is still wet, you can decorate the truffles with edible luster dust, edible glitter, or colored sprinkles if desired.

Chill Again:
- Place the tray back in the refrigerator to allow the marbled chocolate coating to set. This will take about 1-2 hours.

Serve and Enjoy:
- Once the chocolate is fully set, transfer the Marbled Easter Egg Truffles to a serving plate. They are now ready to be enjoyed!

Tips:

- Temperature Control: Work quickly while coating the truffles to ensure the marbled effect sets nicely.
- Storage: Store the truffles in the refrigerator until ready to serve.

These Marbled Easter Egg Truffles not only make a beautiful addition to your Easter festivities but also a delicious treat for everyone to enjoy!

Speckled Easter Egg Cake Pops

Ingredients:

For the Cake Pops:

- 1 baked cake (any flavor), cooled
- 1 cup frosting (cream cheese or buttercream)
- Candy coating or chocolate melts (assorted colors)
- Lollipop sticks or cake pop sticks

For the Speckled Coating:

- 1/4 cup white chocolate chips or candy melts
- Edible food coloring (assorted colors)

For Decorating (Optional):

- Colored sprinkles
- Edible luster dust or edible glitter

Instructions:

For the Cake Pops:

Prepare Cake and Frosting:
- Bake a cake according to your preferred recipe or use a boxed cake mix. Allow it to cool completely. Crumble the cooled cake into fine crumbs. Mix in the frosting until the mixture is moist and holds together.

Shape Cake Balls:
- Take small portions of the cake mixture and roll them into egg shapes. Place the shaped cake balls on a parchment-lined tray.

Insert Sticks:
- Melt a small amount of candy coating or chocolate. Dip the tip of each lollipop stick into the melted coating and insert it into the cake balls. This helps secure the sticks in place.

Chill:
- Place the tray with the cake pops in the refrigerator for about 1 hour to firm up.

For the Speckled Coating:

Melt White Chocolate:
- Melt white chocolate chips or candy melts in the microwave or using a double boiler until smooth.

Color Chocolate:
- Divide the melted white chocolate into separate bowls for each color you want to use. Add a small amount of edible food coloring to each bowl and mix well.

Speckle Effect:
- Dip a clean brush or toothbrush into the colored chocolate and flick it onto the cake pops to create a speckled effect. Repeat with different colors.

Chill Again:
- Place the speckled cake pops back in the refrigerator to allow the chocolate coating to set completely.

For Decorating (Optional):

Additional Decorations:
- If desired, you can further decorate the speckled cake pops with colored sprinkles, edible luster dust, or edible glitter while the chocolate is still wet.

Final Chill:
- Once decorated, place the cake pops back in the refrigerator for a final chill until the coating is fully set.

Serve and Enjoy:
- Once set, your Speckled Easter Egg Cake Pops are ready to be served and enjoyed!

Tips:

- Color Variation: Get creative with different colors for the cake pops and speckles.
- Consistency: Ensure that the cake pop mixture has the right consistency to hold its shape.

These Speckled Easter Egg Cake Pops are not only adorable but also a delicious and festive treat for Easter celebrations!

Easter Egg-Shaped Sugar Cookies

Ingredients:

For the Sugar Cookies:

- 2 3/4 cups all-purpose flour
- 1 teaspoon baking soda
- 1/2 teaspoon baking powder
- 1 cup unsalted butter, softened
- 1 1/2 cups granulated sugar
- 1 large egg
- 1 teaspoon vanilla extract
- 1/2 teaspoon almond extract (optional)
- 1/4 teaspoon salt

For Decorating:

- Royal icing or icing of your choice
- Food coloring (assorted colors)
- Sprinkles and edible decorations

Instructions:

For the Sugar Cookies:

Preheat Oven:
- Preheat your oven to 375°F (190°C). Line baking sheets with parchment paper.

Mix Dry Ingredients:
- In a medium bowl, whisk together the flour, baking soda, baking powder, and salt. Set aside.

Cream Butter and Sugar:
- In a large bowl, cream together the softened butter and granulated sugar until light and fluffy.

Add Egg and Extracts:
- Beat in the egg, vanilla extract, and almond extract (if using), until well combined.

Add Dry Ingredients:
- Gradually add the dry ingredients to the wet ingredients, mixing until just combined. Do not overmix.

Chill Dough:
- Divide the dough in half, shape each half into a disk, wrap in plastic wrap, and refrigerate for at least 1 hour.

Roll and Cut Out Shapes:
- On a floured surface, roll out the chilled dough to about 1/4-inch thickness. Use egg-shaped cookie cutters to cut out cookies and place them on the prepared baking sheets.

Bake:
- Bake in the preheated oven for 8-10 minutes, or until the edges are lightly golden. Allow the cookies to cool on the baking sheets for a few minutes before transferring them to a wire rack to cool completely.

For Decorating:

Prepare Icing:
- Prepare royal icing or your preferred icing according to the package instructions. Divide the icing into different bowls and add food coloring to create various colors.

Decorate:
- Once the cookies are completely cooled, use the colored icing to decorate the Easter egg-shaped cookies. You can create patterns, add lines, or use sprinkles and edible decorations for extra flair.

Allow Icing to Set:
- Allow the icing to set completely before storing or serving the cookies.

Store:
- Store the decorated Easter Egg-Shaped Sugar Cookies in an airtight container at room temperature.

Tips:

- Chill Dough: Chilling the dough helps the cookies hold their shape while baking.
- Icing Consistency: Adjust the consistency of the icing by adding more powdered sugar for thicker icing or more water for thinner icing.

These Easter Egg-Shaped Sugar Cookies are a delightful addition to your Easter festivities, and they're sure to be a hit with family and friends!

Almond Butter Easter Eggs

Ingredients:

For the Almond Butter Filling:

- 1 cup creamy almond butter
- 1/4 cup honey or maple syrup
- 2 tablespoons coconut flour
- 1/2 teaspoon vanilla extract
- 1/4 teaspoon salt

For the Chocolate Coating:

- 1 cup dark chocolate chips or chopped dark chocolate
- 1 tablespoon coconut oil

For Decorating (Optional):

- Pastel-colored candy melts or white chocolate for drizzling
- Sprinkles or edible decorations

Instructions:

For the Almond Butter Filling:

Prepare Almond Butter Mixture:
- In a bowl, combine the creamy almond butter, honey or maple syrup, coconut flour, vanilla extract, and salt. Mix until well combined and a dough-like consistency forms.

Shape Eggs:
- Take small portions of the almond butter mixture and shape them into egg forms. Place the shaped eggs on a parchment-lined tray.

Chill:
- Place the tray with the almond butter eggs in the refrigerator for at least 30 minutes to firm up.

For the Chocolate Coating:

Melt Chocolate:
- In a heatproof bowl, melt the dark chocolate and coconut oil together. You can melt them in the microwave in short intervals or use a double boiler on the stove.

Coat Almond Butter Eggs:

- Using a fork or toothpick, dip each chilled almond butter egg into the melted chocolate, making sure it's fully coated. Allow excess chocolate to drip off.

Place on Tray:
- Place the coated almond butter eggs back on the parchment-lined tray.

Decorate (Optional):
- If desired, melt pastel-colored candy melts or white chocolate and drizzle it over the chocolate-coated almond butter eggs. Quickly add sprinkles or edible decorations before the chocolate sets.

Chill Again:
- Put the tray back in the refrigerator to allow the chocolate coating to set. This will take about 1-2 hours.

Serve and Enjoy:
- Once the chocolate is fully set, your Almond Butter Easter Eggs are ready to be served and enjoyed!

Tips:

- Customize Shapes: Feel free to shape the almond butter mixture into other Easter-themed shapes if desired.
- Storage: Store the almond butter eggs in the refrigerator until ready to serve.

These homemade Almond Butter Easter Eggs are a tasty and healthier alternative to store-bought treats. Enjoy making and sharing them during the Easter season!

Drinks:

Sparkling Raspberry Lemonade

Ingredients:

- 1 cup fresh raspberries
- 1 cup granulated sugar
- 1 cup water
- 1 cup freshly squeezed lemon juice (about 4-6 lemons)
- 4 cups cold sparkling water
- Ice cubes
- Lemon slices and fresh raspberries for garnish
- Mint leaves (optional)

Instructions:

Prepare Raspberry Simple Syrup:
- In a small saucepan, combine the fresh raspberries, granulated sugar, and water. Heat over medium heat, stirring occasionally, until the sugar dissolves and the raspberries break down, creating a syrup. This takes about 5-7 minutes.

Strain the Syrup:
- Strain the raspberry mixture through a fine-mesh sieve into a bowl or pitcher, pressing down to extract as much liquid as possible. Discard the solids and let the syrup cool.

Mix Lemonade:
- In a large pitcher, combine the freshly squeezed lemon juice and the raspberry simple syrup. Stir well to combine.

Add Sparkling Water:
- Just before serving, pour in the cold sparkling water and stir gently to mix.

Serve Over Ice:
- Fill glasses with ice cubes and pour the sparkling raspberry lemonade over the ice.

Garnish:
- Garnish the glasses with lemon slices, fresh raspberries, and mint leaves if desired.

Enjoy:

- Stir before serving, and enjoy the refreshing Sparkling Raspberry Lemonade!

Tips:

- Adjust Sweetness: If you prefer a sweeter lemonade, you can add more raspberry simple syrup to taste.
- Make Ahead: You can prepare the raspberry simple syrup in advance and refrigerate it until you're ready to make the lemonade.

This Sparkling Raspberry Lemonade is perfect for warm days, gatherings, or as a special treat for yourself. Enjoy!

Easter Punch with Fruit Ice Ring

Ingredients:

For the Fruit Ice Ring:

- Assorted fresh fruits (such as berries, citrus slices, and melon balls)
- Mint leaves (optional)
- 1-2 cups cold water

For the Easter Punch:

- 2 cups pineapple juice
- 1 cup orange juice
- 1/2 cup cranberry juice
- 1 liter ginger ale or lemon-lime soda, chilled
- 1/4 cup grenadine syrup
- Ice cubes

Instructions:

For the Fruit Ice Ring:

Prepare Fruits:
- Wash and slice the assorted fresh fruits. Arrange them in a Bundt pan or a ring-shaped mold. Add mint leaves for extra freshness and color.

Add Water:
- Pour cold water into the pan, covering the fruits. Make sure not to overfill; you want the water to freeze around the fruits.

Freeze:
- Place the Bundt pan in the freezer and let it freeze completely. This can take several hours or overnight.

Release Ice Ring:
- Once fully frozen, run the bottom of the pan under warm water for a few seconds to release the ice ring. Place the fruit ice ring in a punch bowl.

For the Easter Punch:

Mix Fruit Punch:
- In a large pitcher, combine pineapple juice, orange juice, cranberry juice, and grenadine syrup. Stir well to mix.

Chill:
- Refrigerate the fruit punch mixture until it's thoroughly chilled.

Assemble Punch Bowl:
- Just before serving, place the fruit ice ring in the punch bowl. Pour the chilled fruit punch mixture over the ice ring.

Add Carbonation:
- Gently pour the ginger ale or lemon-lime soda over the fruit punch mixture to add carbonation.

Serve:
- Stir the punch gently. Ladle the Easter Punch into glasses filled with ice cubes.

Garnish:
- Garnish individual glasses with additional fruit slices or mint leaves if desired.

Enjoy:
- Enjoy the refreshing Easter Punch with family and friends!

Tips:

- Customize Fruits: Feel free to customize the fruit selection based on your preferences and what's in season.
- Make it Adult: For an adult version, you can add a splash of your favorite spirit like vodka or champagne.

This Easter Punch with a Fruit Ice Ring is not only delicious but also makes a beautiful centerpiece for your Easter celebration!

Minty Lime Cooler

Ingredients:

- 1 cup fresh lime juice (about 8-10 limes)
- 1/2 cup fresh mint leaves, plus extra for garnish
- 1/2 cup granulated sugar (adjust to taste)
- 4 cups cold water
- Ice cubes
- Lime slices for garnish

Instructions:

Prepare Mint Syrup:
- In a small saucepan, combine the fresh mint leaves, granulated sugar, and 1 cup of water. Heat over medium heat, stirring until the sugar dissolves. Allow it to simmer for a few minutes to infuse the mint flavor. Remove from heat and let it cool.

Strain Mint Syrup:
- Strain the mint syrup through a fine-mesh sieve to remove the mint leaves. You now have mint-infused syrup.

Mix Lime Juice:
- In a large pitcher, combine the fresh lime juice and the mint-infused syrup.

Add Cold Water:
- Pour in the cold water and stir well to mix.

Adjust Sweetness:
- Taste the Minty Lime Cooler and adjust the sweetness by adding more sugar if needed. Stir until the sugar is fully dissolved.

Chill:
- Refrigerate the Minty Lime Cooler for at least 1-2 hours to let the flavors meld.

Serve Over Ice:
- Fill glasses with ice cubes and pour the Minty Lime Cooler over the ice.

Garnish:
- Garnish each glass with a slice of lime and a sprig of fresh mint.

Enjoy:
- Stir before drinking and enjoy the refreshing Minty Lime Cooler!

Tips:

- Mint Intensity: If you prefer a stronger mint flavor, you can muddle the mint leaves before adding them to the sugar and water mixture.
- Make it Sparkling: For a fizzy version, you can top the Minty Lime Cooler with sparkling water or soda just before serving.

This Minty Lime Cooler is perfect for warm days or as a delightful non-alcoholic option for any occasion. Cheers!

Carrot Orange Ginger Smoothie

Ingredients:

- 1 cup carrots, peeled and chopped
- 1 large orange, peeled and segmented
- 1/2-inch piece of fresh ginger, peeled and grated
- 1 banana, peeled
- 1 cup plain Greek yogurt
- 1 cup ice cubes
- 1-2 tablespoons honey or maple syrup (optional, for sweetness)
- 1/2 cup cold water or orange juice (adjust for desired consistency)

Instructions:

Prepare Ingredients:
- Wash, peel, and chop the carrots. Peel and segment the orange. Peel and grate the fresh ginger.

Assemble Blender:
- In a blender, combine the chopped carrots, orange segments, grated ginger, banana, Greek yogurt, and ice cubes.

Add Sweetener (Optional):
- If you prefer a sweeter smoothie, add honey or maple syrup to the blender.

Pour Liquid:
- Pour in the cold water or orange juice to help with blending. Adjust the amount based on your desired smoothie consistency.

Blend:
- Blend all the ingredients until smooth and creamy. If needed, stop and scrape down the sides of the blender to ensure all ingredients are well incorporated.

Taste and Adjust:
- Taste the smoothie and adjust the sweetness or thickness by adding more honey, water, or orange juice if necessary.

Serve:
- Pour the Carrot Orange Ginger Smoothie into glasses.

Garnish (Optional):
- Garnish with a slice of orange or a sprinkle of grated ginger for an extra touch.

Enjoy:
- Enjoy the refreshing and nutritious Carrot Orange Ginger Smoothie!

Tips:

- Frozen Ingredients: You can use frozen banana or add more ice cubes for a colder and thicker smoothie.
- Nutritional Boost: Consider adding a scoop of protein powder or a handful of spinach for an extra nutritional boost.

This smoothie is not only delicious but also packed with vitamins and antioxidants. It's a perfect choice for a healthy and energizing drink!

Non-Alcoholic Easter Egg Punch

Ingredients:

For the Punch:

- 2 cups pineapple juice
- 2 cups orange juice
- 1 cup cranberry juice
- 1 liter ginger ale or lemon-lime soda, chilled
- 1/4 cup grenadine syrup (optional, for sweetness and color)
- Ice cubes

For the Easter Egg Ice Cubes:

- Assorted fruit juices (such as orange, cranberry, or raspberry)
- Water

For Garnish:

- Fresh fruit slices (lemons, oranges, berries)
- Mint leaves (optional)

Instructions:

For the Easter Egg Ice Cubes:

Prepare Fruit Juices:
- Pour assorted fruit juices into separate containers. You can use different colors and flavors for variety.

Fill Ice Cube Trays:
- Pour the fruit juices into Easter egg-shaped ice cube trays. Fill each section with a different juice to create colorful ice cubes. Freeze until solid.

For the Non-Alcoholic Easter Egg Punch:

Prepare Easter Egg Ice Cubes:
- Once the Easter egg-shaped ice cubes are frozen, remove them from the trays.

Assemble Punch:

- In a large punch bowl or pitcher, combine pineapple juice, orange juice, cranberry juice, and grenadine syrup if using.

Add Easter Egg Ice Cubes:
- Place the Easter egg-shaped ice cubes into the punch.

Pour Chilled Soda:
- Just before serving, pour the chilled ginger ale or lemon-lime soda over the punch. Stir gently.

Garnish:
- Garnish the punch with fresh fruit slices and mint leaves for a festive touch.

Serve:
- Serve the Non-Alcoholic Easter Egg Punch over ice.

Enjoy:
- Enjoy this colorful and refreshing punch with family and friends!

Tips:

- Adjust Sweetness: Taste the punch before adding grenadine syrup and adjust the sweetness to your liking.
- Fruit Variations: Experiment with different fruit juices and combinations for the Easter egg-shaped ice cubes.

This Non-Alcoholic Easter Egg Punch is a fun and family-friendly addition to your Easter celebration, perfect for all ages to enjoy!

Quiche Lorraine

Ingredients:

For the Pie Crust:

- 1 1/4 cups all-purpose flour
- 1/2 cup unsalted butter, cold and cut into small pieces
- 1/4 teaspoon salt
- 2-4 tablespoons ice water

For the Filling:

- 8 slices bacon, cooked and crumbled
- 1 cup shredded Gruyere or Swiss cheese
- 1/4 cup finely chopped onion
- 1 1/2 cups heavy cream
- 4 large eggs
- 1/4 teaspoon salt
- 1/4 teaspoon black pepper
- 1/4 teaspoon ground nutmeg

Instructions:

For the Pie Crust:

Prepare Pie Crust:
- In a food processor, combine the flour, cold butter, and salt. Pulse until the mixture resembles coarse crumbs.

Add Ice Water:
- With the food processor running, gradually add ice water, one tablespoon at a time, until the dough comes together and forms a ball.

Chill Dough:
- Flatten the dough into a disc, wrap it in plastic wrap, and refrigerate for at least 1 hour.

Roll Out Dough:
- Preheat the oven to 375°F (190°C). Roll out the chilled dough on a floured surface and fit it into a 9-inch pie dish. Trim any excess dough and crimp the edges. Prick the bottom of the crust with a fork.

Blind Bake:

- Line the pie crust with parchment paper and fill it with pie weights or dried beans. Blind bake for 15 minutes. Remove the weights and parchment paper, then bake for an additional 5 minutes until the crust is golden. Set aside.

For the Filling:

Preheat Oven:
- Reduce the oven temperature to 350°F (175°C).

Prepare Filling:
- In a bowl, whisk together the heavy cream, eggs, salt, pepper, and nutmeg.

Assemble Quiche:
- Sprinkle the crumbled bacon, shredded cheese, and chopped onion evenly over the baked pie crust. Pour the egg mixture over the top.

Bake:
- Bake in the preheated oven for 30-35 minutes or until the quiche is set and golden brown on top.

Cool and Serve:
- Allow the Quiche Lorraine to cool for a few minutes before slicing. Serve warm.

Tips:

- Make-Ahead: You can prepare the pie crust and filling a day in advance, refrigerate them separately, and assemble and bake the quiche just before serving.
- Variations: Feel free to customize the quiche by adding other ingredients like sautéed mushrooms, spinach, or diced tomatoes.

Quiche Lorraine is a versatile and delicious dish that can be enjoyed for brunch, lunch, or dinner. Enjoy!

Blueberry Pancakes

Ingredients:

- 1 cup all-purpose flour
- 2 tablespoons granulated sugar
- 1 teaspoon baking powder
- 1/2 teaspoon baking soda
- 1/4 teaspoon salt
- 3/4 cup buttermilk
- 1/4 cup milk
- 1 large egg
- 2 tablespoons unsalted butter, melted
- 1 cup fresh or frozen blueberries
- Butter or cooking spray for greasing the griddle

Instructions:

Preheat Griddle or Pan:
- Preheat a griddle or non-stick skillet over medium heat.

Mix Dry Ingredients:
- In a large mixing bowl, whisk together the flour, sugar, baking powder, baking soda, and salt.

Combine Wet Ingredients:
- In a separate bowl, whisk together the buttermilk, milk, egg, and melted butter.

Combine Wet and Dry Ingredients:
- Pour the wet ingredients into the dry ingredients and stir until just combined. It's okay if there are a few lumps.

Fold in Blueberries:
- Gently fold in the blueberries until evenly distributed throughout the batter.

Grease Griddle:
- Lightly grease the griddle or skillet with butter or cooking spray.

Scoop Batter onto Griddle:
- Using a 1/4 cup measuring cup, scoop the batter onto the hot griddle, spacing the pancakes apart.

Cook Until Bubbles Form:
- Cook the pancakes until bubbles form on the surface, and the edges start to look set.

Flip and Cook Other Side:

- Carefully flip the pancakes with a spatula and cook the other side until golden brown.

Serve Warm:
- Transfer the cooked pancakes to a plate and keep warm. Repeat the process with the remaining batter.

Serve with Toppings:
- Serve the Blueberry Pancakes warm with maple syrup, additional blueberries, and a pat of butter if desired.

Tips:

- Fresh vs. Frozen Blueberries: If using frozen blueberries, you can add them directly to the batter without thawing, but be aware that they may slightly discolor the batter.

These Blueberry Pancakes are a delightful breakfast treat, perfect for a lazy weekend morning or any day you crave a sweet and fruity breakfast!

Eggs Benedict with Hollandaise Sauce

Ingredients:

For the Hollandaise Sauce:

- 3 large egg yolks
- 1 tablespoon lemon juice
- 1/2 cup unsalted butter, melted
- Salt and cayenne pepper to taste

For the Eggs Benedict:

- 4 large eggs
- 4 English muffins, split and toasted
- 8 slices Canadian bacon or ham
- Chopped fresh chives or parsley for garnish (optional)
- Salt and black pepper to taste

Instructions:

For the Hollandaise Sauce:

　Prepare Double Boiler:
- Fill a saucepan with a couple of inches of water and bring it to a simmer. Place a heatproof bowl over the simmering water, ensuring that the bottom of the bowl doesn't touch the water.

　Whisk Egg Yolks:
- In the heatproof bowl, whisk the egg yolks and lemon juice until well combined.

　Cook Egg Yolks:
- Continue whisking over the simmering water until the mixture thickens, about 2-3 minutes. Be careful not to scramble the eggs.

　Add Melted Butter:
- Slowly drizzle in the melted butter while whisking constantly until the sauce thickens. Remove from heat.

　Season:
- Season the Hollandaise sauce with salt and cayenne pepper to taste. Keep the sauce warm while you prepare the rest of the dish.

For the Eggs Benedict:

Poach Eggs:
- Poach the eggs by bringing a pot of water to a gentle simmer. Crack each egg into a small bowl and carefully slide it into the simmering water. Cook for about 3-4 minutes for a soft poached egg.

Cook Canadian Bacon or Ham:
- While the eggs are poaching, heat a skillet over medium heat and cook the Canadian bacon or ham until lightly browned on both sides.

Assemble Eggs Benedict:
- Place toasted English muffin halves on a plate. Top each half with a slice of Canadian bacon or ham, followed by a poached egg.

Pour Hollandaise Sauce:
- Spoon a generous amount of Hollandaise sauce over each poached egg.

Garnish:
- Garnish with chopped fresh chives or parsley if desired. Season with salt and black pepper to taste.

Serve Immediately:
- Serve Eggs Benedict immediately while the Hollandaise sauce is warm.

Tips:

- Keep it Warm: If the Hollandaise sauce thickens too much or cools, you can place it over the warm water again and whisk until it reaches the desired consistency.
- Variations: Feel free to add a slice of smoked salmon or sautéed spinach for variations.

Eggs Benedict with Hollandaise Sauce is a decadent brunch classic that never fails to impress. Enjoy!

Smoked Salmon Bagels

Ingredients:

- 4 bagels, sliced and toasted
- 8 oz (about 225g) smoked salmon
- 1/2 cup cream cheese, softened
- 1 tablespoon capers, drained
- Red onion, thinly sliced
- Fresh dill, for garnish
- Lemon wedges, for serving
- Salt and black pepper, to taste

Instructions:

Prepare Bagels:
- Slice the bagels in half and toast them until they are golden brown.

Spread Cream Cheese:
- Spread a generous layer of softened cream cheese on each half of the toasted bagels.

Layer Smoked Salmon:
- Place a few slices of smoked salmon on top of the cream cheese, covering the entire surface of the bagel.

Add Toppings:
- Sprinkle capers over the smoked salmon. Add thinly sliced red onions for a burst of flavor.

Season:
- Season with salt and black pepper to taste.

Garnish:
- Garnish with fresh dill for a pop of color and added freshness.

Serve with Lemon Wedges:
- Serve the smoked salmon bagels with lemon wedges on the side. Squeezing a bit of fresh lemon juice over the smoked salmon adds brightness to the dish.

Enjoy:
- Serve immediately and enjoy your delicious Smoked Salmon Bagels!

Tips:

- Variations: Customize your smoked salmon bagels with additional toppings such as sliced tomatoes, cucumber, or avocado.
- Herb Cream Cheese: Consider using flavored cream cheese, such as dill or chive cream cheese, for an extra layer of flavor.

Smoked Salmon Bagels are not only a classic brunch option but also a perfect choice for special occasions. Enjoy your delightful and savory breakfast!

Fruit Salad with Honey-Lime Dressing

Ingredients:

For the Honey-Lime Dressing:

- 3 tablespoons honey
- 2 tablespoons fresh lime juice
- 1 teaspoon lime zest
- 1 tablespoon fresh orange juice (optional)
- 1 tablespoon chopped fresh mint (optional)

For the Fruit Salad:

- 2 cups fresh strawberries, hulled and halved
- 1 cup fresh blueberries
- 1 cup fresh pineapple, diced
- 1 cup green grapes, halved
- 1 cup mango, diced
- 1 cup kiwi, peeled and sliced
- 1 banana, sliced (add just before serving)
- Fresh mint leaves for garnish (optional)

Instructions:

For the Honey-Lime Dressing:

Prepare Dressing:
- In a small bowl, whisk together honey, lime juice, lime zest, and optional orange juice until well combined.

Add Mint (Optional):
- If using mint, stir in the chopped fresh mint into the dressing. This adds a delightful herbaceous flavor.

Set Aside:
- Set the dressing aside to allow the flavors to meld while you prepare the fruit.

For the Fruit Salad:

Prepare Fruit:
- In a large mixing bowl, combine strawberries, blueberries, pineapple, grapes, mango, and kiwi.

Drizzle Dressing:

- Drizzle the honey-lime dressing over the fruit. Gently toss the fruit salad to ensure that all the fruits are coated with the dressing.

Chill (Optional):
- Refrigerate the fruit salad for about 15-30 minutes to let the flavors mingle. This step is optional but enhances the taste.

Add Banana (Before Serving):
- Just before serving, add sliced bananas to the fruit salad and gently toss. Adding bananas at the end helps prevent them from browning too quickly.

Garnish:
- Garnish with fresh mint leaves if desired.

Serve:
- Serve the Fruit Salad with Honey-Lime Dressing in a bowl or individual servings.

Tips:

- Variations: Feel free to use any combination of your favorite fruits. Other options include oranges, raspberries, blackberries, or peaches.
- Make-Ahead: You can prepare the dressing and chop the fruits ahead of time, but it's best to assemble the salad just before serving to maintain freshness.

This Fruit Salad with Honey-Lime Dressing is a delightful and colorful way to enjoy a variety of fresh fruits. It's perfect for breakfast, brunch, or as a refreshing side dish.

Enjoy!

Fruit Salad with Honey-Lime Dressing

Ingredients:

For the Honey-Lime Dressing:

- 3 tablespoons honey
- 2 tablespoons fresh lime juice
- 1 teaspoon lime zest
- 1 tablespoon fresh orange juice (optional)
- 1 tablespoon chopped fresh mint (optional)

For the Fruit Salad:

- 2 cups fresh strawberries, hulled and halved
- 1 cup fresh blueberries
- 1 cup fresh pineapple, diced
- 1 cup green grapes, halved
- 1 cup mango, diced
- 1 cup kiwi, peeled and sliced
- 1 banana, sliced (add just before serving)

- Fresh mint leaves for garnish (optional)

Instructions:

For the Honey-Lime Dressing:

- Prepare Dressing:
    - In a small bowl, whisk together honey, lime juice, lime zest, and optional orange juice until well combined.
- Add Mint (Optional):
    - If using mint, stir in the chopped fresh mint into the dressing. This adds a delightful herbaceous flavor.
- Set Aside:
    - Set the dressing aside to allow the flavors to meld while you prepare the fruit.

For the Fruit Salad:

- Prepare Fruit:
    - In a large mixing bowl, combine strawberries, blueberries, pineapple, grapes, mango, and kiwi.
- Drizzle Dressing:
    - Drizzle the honey-lime dressing over the fruit. Gently toss the fruit salad to ensure that all the fruits are coated with the dressing.
- Chill (Optional):
    - Refrigerate the fruit salad for about 15-30 minutes to let the flavors mingle. This step is optional but enhances the taste.
- Add Banana (Before Serving):
    - Just before serving, add sliced bananas to the fruit salad and gently toss. Adding bananas at the end helps prevent them from browning too quickly.
- Garnish:
    - Garnish with fresh mint leaves if desired.
- Serve:
    - Serve the Fruit Salad with Honey-Lime Dressing in a bowl or individual servings.

Tips:

- Variations: Feel free to use any combination of your favorite fruits. Other options include oranges, raspberries, blackberries, or peaches.
- Make-Ahead: You can prepare the dressing and chop the fruits ahead of time, but it's best to assemble the salad just before serving to maintain freshness.

This Fruit Salad with Honey-Lime Dressing is a delightful and colorful way to enjoy a variety of fresh fruits. It's perfect for breakfast, brunch, or as a refreshing side dish. Enjoy!